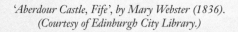

'Aberdour Castle, Fife', by Mary Webster (1836).
(Courtesy of Edinburgh City Library.)

Michael Apted

EDITED BY CHRIS TABRAHAM
ILLUSTRATED BY DAVID SIMON
PHOTOGRAPHY BY HISTORIC SCOTLAND PHOTOGRAPHIC UNIT
PRINTED IN SCOTLAND FROM SUSTAINABLE MATERIAL
BY BUCCLEUCH PRINTERS LTD., HAWICK

FIRST PUBLISHED BY HMSO 1961
THIS REVISED EDITION FIRST PUBLISHED BY HISTORIC SCOTLAND 1996
CROWN COPYRIGHT © HISTORIC SCOTLAND 1996
REPRINTED 2007
ISBN 1 900168 21 9

INTRODUCTION

"...by reason of his great age and estate
he must have certain servitors to wait
upon him for keeping of his person,
houses and strengths, and especially
of his strength and fortalice of Aberdour,
lying on the coast side."

(FROM A LICENCE EXEMPTING JAMES DOUGLAS,
THIRD EARL OF MORTON, FROM MILITARY
SERVICE AGAINST ENGLAND IN 1547.)

Aberdour Castle was probably begun around 1200 by the de Mortimer family. After a brief period in the ownership of the Randolph family, in 1342 it passed to the Douglases, and has remained with them ever since, though it was not until 1642 that it became the principal seat of the branch of the family whose head was created Earl of Morton in 1456. The Mortons were closely connected to the Crown. From 1572 to 1578 the fourth Earl served as Regent for the young James VI, and the sixth Earl is best known for having served as custodian of Mary Queen of Scots during her term of imprisonment in Lochleven Castle in 1567-8. The support of the seventh Earl for Charles I during the Civil War led to the sale of many of the Morton lands, and as a result the Earl came to live at Aberdour. The castle was abandoned as a residence by the Morton family in 1725 when they moved to nearby Aberdour House, though the place continued in use for another 200 years.

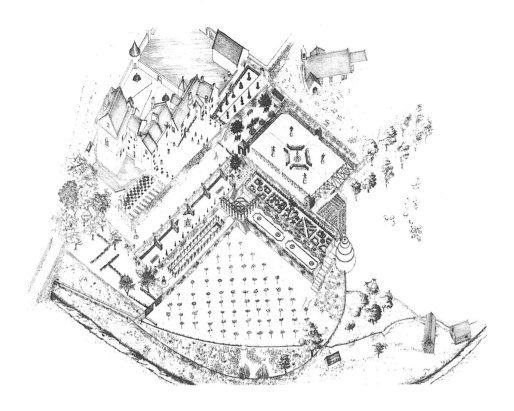

An impression of how Aberdour Castle and gardens might have looked about 1650, drawn by John Knight.

The castle today illustrates how a medieval castle could be extended and modified over several centuries. First built to provide its owner with a secure place of strength, it was later extended in several stages until it became an extensive, outward-looking residence surrounded by delightful pleasure-grounds. As such it tells a great deal about changes in architectural and domestic fashions, as well as about the developing fortunes of the families who owned it.

THE STORY OF ABERDOUR CASTLE

THE DE MORTIMERS AND THE FIRST CASTLE

*L*ittle is known about the early owners of Aberdour. The barony seems to have been acquired by Alan de Mortimer in the early twelfth century, and it was probably under his auspices that the parish church, dedicated to St Fillan, was built. Another Alan Mortimer is referred to in 1216, in connection with a grant of a part of his estate to the Augustinian abbey on nearby Inchcolm Island. It may have been this Alan who had the hall house built which forms part of the present tower house. What happened next is unclear. Either the Mortimer line died out or they supported the wrong side during the first 'War of Independence' for in about 1325 King Robert the Bruce granted the lands to his nephew, Thomas Randolph, Earl of Moray. In 1342 Moray's younger son granted the property to Sir William Douglas, popularly known as the 'Flower of Chivalry', and it has remained with one branch or another of the Douglas family ever since.

An impression of how the first castle (the hall house) might have looked from the south east about 1200, drawn by Harry Bland.

The interior of St Fillan's, Aberdour, looking east.

ABERDOUR AND THE DOUGLASES

Sir William Douglas added to his estates the lordship of Liddesdale, on the English Border, and the barony of Dalkeith. In 1351 he granted the lands of Aberdour to his nephew, James, later Lord of Dalkeith, and the confirmation by David II in 1361 of this transaction contains the earliest known reference to Aberdour Castle which Sir William reserved to himself. In 1386 the baronies of Aberdour and Dalkeith were united into a single barony of regality, the regality of Dalkeith, an arrangement which lasted until 1642. Dalkeith served as the main seat and Aberdour as a secondary residence.

James died of influenza in 1420 and was succeeded by his son, James, who had married Elizabeth, a daughter of Robert III. Their son, also James, succeeded about 1440, but in 1441 Parliament declared him insane. His father-in-law was constituted his curator and appointed custodian of Aberdour and Dalkeith.

James, third Lord Dalkeith, succeeded between 1456-8 and in anticipation of his marriage to Joanna, deaf and dumb daughter of James I, was created Earl of Morton; the name derived from the lands of Morton near East Calder. In 1474 his cousin, Hugh, renounced his claims to the title, and so the quarrel between James' father and uncle was finally resolved in the Earl's favour. Thereafter the first and second Earls remained in peaceful occupation of *"the village, mill, castle and fortalice of Aberdour"*.

The third Earl succeeded about 1513, the same year as King James V. But in 1538 he and his wife were summoned by the Crown for non-payment of their feudal dues on Aberdour. The King's action was probably prompted by his wish to have the Morton lands for himself, an objective he achieved in 1540 by banishing the Earl to Inverness. The Earl, by now in poor health, travelled as far as Brechin and there resigned his lands in favour of his kinsman, Robert Douglas of Lochleven. The latter, acting under compulsion, resigned them to the King with the exception of Aberdour which he was allowed to keep.

On James V's death in 1542, the unjust settlement of Brechin was quickly overturned. To secure this end the Earl enlisted the aid of another kinsman, George Douglas of Pittendreich, at the price of a marriage contract between his youngest daughter, Elizabeth, and Sir George's second son, James, who was to succeed to the earldom on the Earl's death. The Earl may also have been helped to re-establish his position by the Lord Governor, James, Earl of Arran, for in December 1542 John Hamilton of Milnburn was reimbursed for travelling to Aberdour *"with certain silver work of my Lord Governor to be delivered to the Earl of Morton in pledge of a sum of money borrowed from the said Earl"*. Five years later another messenger, Alexander Guthrie, was paid for the hire of a boat to Aberdour and back *"he being sent to my Lord of Morton afore his decease to inquire for certain pledges of my Lord Governors laid in pleadge to the said Earl"*.

In 1544 war broke out with England. The Earl was granted exemption from military service on the grounds that he was *"of great age, sickly and tender of complexion, so that he may not endure and sustain pain and travail of wars without danger to his life"*. He died in 1548.

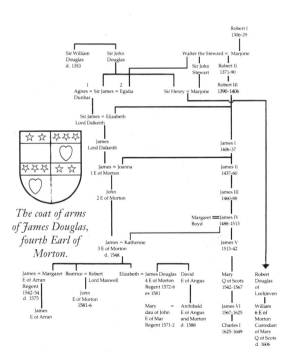

The coat of arms of James Douglas, fourth Earl of Morton.

The royal connections of the Douglases of Morton.

REGENT MORTON

The third Earl was succeeded by his son-in-law, James Douglas, known to history as the Regent Morton. However, under the 1542 settlement, the barony of Aberdour had been reserved to the late Earl's wife, the Countess Katherine, during her lifetime. The Aberdour lands were still in her hands in 1553 when Morton obtained discharge of a precept by the Countess calling the tenants of Aberdour and other lands to her own court of justice away from the regality of Dalkeith. In 1564 Morton obtained confirmation of his right to the whole barony when Queen Mary formally annulled the resignation made by James, the third Earl, *"under fear for his life"*.

On 9 March 1566 Riccio was murdered at Holyrood, and although not one of the assassins, Morton, then Chancellor, was regarded as one of the principal conspirators. On 19 March a herald and a messenger were sent from Edinburgh with letters *"to search, seek, intromet and make inventory of part of the escheit goods, corns, cattle and others whatsoever which pertained to James, Earl of Morton, being in Aberdour"*. The charges subsequently brought were that Morton and others were *"complices in the crewell murthering and slaying of umquhile David Riccio thair majesteis domesticall servitor, and detaining of their highnesses persons in captivity within the Palace of Holyroodhouse"*. The summons were delivered at Dalkeith and Aberdour in vain, for Morton had fled to England.

The storm blew over quickly and by Christmas 1566 Morton was back home and in favour once more. Within the year Mary was a prisoner in Lochleven Castle, where

James Douglas, fourth Earl of Morton; a painting attributed to Arnold Brockhorst. (Courtesy of the National Galleries of Scotland.)

The pair of windows lighting the inner chambers of Morton and Lady Elizabeth's private apartments in the central range.

on 24 July 1567 Morton and others received her abdication in favour of her infant son. James VI's coronation took place at Stirling a week later, and Morton took the oath "*inclinand his body and layand his hand on the buike of God, in name and upoon the behalf of his Grace*".

Morton was appointed Regent in 1572, a position he retained until 1578. On at least one occasion, in August 1576, the Privy Council met at Aberdour, where they would doubtless have admired Morton's newly completed residence and terraced garden.

It was from Aberdour that Morton wrote in March 1580 to warn his kinsman, the laird of Lochleven, that he had been summoned to Stirling in connection with a plot to surprise the King. If this was an attempt to implicate Morton it failed, but in January of the following year he was imprisoned first in Edinburgh then in Dumbarton, "*being suspected and accused as culpable of the treasonable murder of umquhile the king our Sovereign Lord's father*" ~ that is, Henry Lord Darnley, Queen Mary's second husband. The result of Morton's trial was foregone, and despite lack of proof he was convicted and executed.

ABERDOUR AND THE LATER EARLS OF MORTON

Whilst Morton was in prison, his lands had been transferred to the custody of his nephew, Archibald, eighth Earl of Angus, but after his execution they were granted to one of his principal enemies, the Earl of Lennox. In 1587, however, Lennox restored them to Angus, as the heir of entail, *"for the sake of peace in the realm amongst the nobles of the same"*. On Angus's death in 1588, Sir William Douglas of Lochleven, Queen Mary's jailer during her time there, was created sixth Earl of Morton.

By the time of Douglas' death in 1606, his eldest son was also dead. He had travelled abroad in 1584 and it seems he was captured by the Turks and died in prison in Algiers. His wife, Jean Lyon, subsequently married Alexander Lindsay, Lord Spynie. Lord Spynie is said to have lived at Aberdour until his untimely death in an Edinburgh street brawl in 1607.

William Douglas, seventh Earl of Morton. (Courtesy of the National Galleries of Scotland.)

THE MORTON FAMILY HOME

The sixth Earl was succeeded by his grandson, also William, a prominent supporter of the Stewarts and Lord Treasurer of Scotland from 1630-6. However, having spent much of his fortune in the royal interest, in 1642 he was forced to dispose of Dalkeith, the chief family seat, to the Earl of Buccleuch, and take up residence at Aberdour. As some compensation for his losses Charles I gave him a charter of the Earldom of Orkney and Shetland, a holding which remained with the family until 1766. It was during the seventh Earl's time that the eastern part of the castle, including the gallery, was built, probably before he was forced to sell Dalkeith.

The sundial on the east range, bearing the initials of William, seventh Earl of Morton, and Countess Anne, his wife.

The initials of William, seventh Earl of Morton, above the window lighting his new gallery in the east range.

An inventory of the contents of Aberdour, made in 1647, shows the layout of the castle and the way in which it was furnished in its heyday. The rooms listed are:

The dining room,
My Lord's chamber,
the gallery,
the gallery chamber,
Mr Wm. Douglas chamber,
Ard. Douglas chamber,
the cabinet,
the tower chamber,

the tower head,
the chancellor's chamber,
the pantry,
the meat hall,
the yett chamber,
the porter lodge,
the stable and chamber loft,
Wm. Ros' chamber,

the inner woman house,
the outer woman house,
the girnal house,
the old meat hall,
the brew house,
the bake house

The castle was also richly furnished. The walls of the principal rooms were hung with tapestry and had curtains at the windows. The main features of the private rooms were the great beds, one of red silk with gold fringes, another of red cloth with black and yellow lace. There was a billiard table in the tower chamber and the upper wardrobe contained a *"hamper full of trash"*

THE END OF A NOBLE HOUSE

Earl William died in 1648, to be succeeded by his son Robert, who died he following year, and his grandson William, the ninth Earl. The latter granted a licence to his aunt, Lady Kinnoul, "*to repair to our house and castle of Aberdour with her children and family and there to inhabit and remain*". An inventory of 1675 shows the castle in decline.

The surviving rentals from this period give an insight into the running of the house. These record the names of successive chamberlains and of the humbler folk - Elspeth Henderson who "*kept the house*" in 1683, "*your servant Margaret*", John Grant, stabler, Robert Adam, gardener, and a host of others. There are the estate workers, the blacksmith, the mason, even the periwig maker.

The accounts record expenditure from the Earl's funeral to the cost of drinks supplied to the men on Lord Aberdour's birthday. They list the mendicants required by the horses, such as brandy for a stroke, to the longer list of healing plasters, purging potions, pectoral pills and balsams provided for the family in 1744 by James Kirkland, Surgeon Apothecarie in Edinburgh.

The records also contain a good deal of information about the development and stocking of the garden, one of the chief delights of Aberdour. In 1650 Anne Murray, later Lady Halkett, wrote "*I was led in through the garden, which was so fragrant and delightful that I thought I was still in England*". This garden was probably the walled garden built in the 1630s.

The castle is traditionally believed to have been destroyed by fire in 1715 when occupied by Hanoverian dragoons during the Jacobite Rising. In fact, the place had been badly damaged by fire before 1700. In 1690 James Smith, master mason, surveyed the castle and provided detailed estimates for its repair. This included the building of a new two-storeyed mansion to the north of the gallery. The plan was not adopted and only a minor repair of the east range was carried out. By 1703 the refurbishment was completed as John Phin and Christian Alan cleaned the whole house, brushed the pictures in the gallery and carried away the rubbish at the entry to the house.

The reconstruction of the central and west ranges was apparently not even considered; on the contrary the Earl went so far as to secure "*an account of what is thought of as expenses to take down the castle of Aberdour all bewest the gallery and the woman house (laundry) and the inner court dyke*". But the cost was beyond his means and the ruins were left to crumble. In the end the family chose not to restore or rebuild the castle but instead acquired the adjoining property, then known as Cuttlehill, now Aberdour House. The rebuilt east range continued in use as barrack, school room, masonic hall and dwelling until in 1924 the castle was placed in State care.

A SHORT TOUR OF

1. OUTER AND INNER COURTYARDS

AREAS ENCLOSED BY DEFENSIVE WALLS THROUGH
WHICH THOSE ENTERING THE CASTLE HAD TO
PASS. THE WALLS ARE NOW LARGELY REDUCED TO
THEIR FOUNDATIONS, BUT THE OUTER ENTRANCE
GATE WAS DISMANTLED WHEN THE RAILWAY WAS
CUT THROUGH IN 1890 AND RE-ERECTED AT THE
END OF THE PRESENT MODERN APPROACH. THE
INNER COURTYARD CONTAINED A WELL.

2. TOWER HOUSE

BUILT AS A TWO-STOREYED HALL HOUSE ABOUT
1200, BUT RAISED IN HEIGHT AND ALTERED
INTERNALLY IN THE 15TH CENTURY TO CREATE A
TOWER HOUSE, WITH SERVICE ROOMS AT GROUND
LEVEL, A HALL IN THE MIDDLE AND PRIVATE
CHAMBERS AT THE TOP. MOST OF THE TOWER
HOUSE COLLAPSED IN THE 19TH CENTURY.

3. CENTRAL RANGE

BUILT MOST PROBABLY BY REGENT MORTON ABOUT
1550 AS A NEW RESIDENCE TO REPLACE THE
CRAMPED ROOMS IN THE TOWER HOUSE [2]. ABOVE
A GROUND-FLOOR KITCHEN AND STORE WERE TWO
FLOORS, EACH CONTAINING A THREE-ROOMED
APARTMENT, ONE FOR THE EARL AND THE OTHER
FOR HIS COUNTESS. A PRIVATE STAIR ON THE SOUTH
GAVE ACCESS TO THE TERRACED GARDEN [6].

4. SERVICE COURTYARD

A BACK COURT CONTAINING ANCILLARY BUILDINGS,
INCLUDING A BAKEHOUSE AND A BREWHOUSE.

5. EAST RANGE

THE LAST MAJOR ADDITION TO THE CASTLE, BUILT
FOR THE 7TH EARL IN THE EARLY 17TH CENTURY. IT
HOUSED A PICTURE GALLERY ON THE UPPER FLOOR
OF THE MAIN BLOCK WITH A STABLE BENEATH, AND
PRIVATE CHAMBERS IN THE PROJECTING WING AT
THE SOUTH-EAST CORNER. THE PITCHED ROOF
OVER THE GALLERY IS A LATER ALTERATION.

BERDOUR CASTLE

6. TERRACED GARDEN

MOST PROBABLY LAID OUT IN THE 1550s AS PART OF REGENT MORTON'S BUILDING PROGRAMME TO IMPROVE HIS HOUSE. FOUR TERRACES, LINKED BY STONE STEPS, CASCADE DOWN TO A LEVEL AREA OF GROUND WHICH WAS LAID OUT AS AN ORCHARD IN 1690. THE BEEHIVE-SHAPED DOVECOT WAS PROBABLY BUILT LATER IN THE SIXTEENTH CENTURY. BEYOND THE DOVECOT, BESIDE THE DOUR BURN, IS THE REMAINS OF THE NETHER MILL OF ABERDOUR.

7. WALLED GARDEN

BUILT FOR THE 7TH EARL IN THE 1630s TO COMPLEMENT HIS NEW EAST RANGE [5]. AT THE SOUTH-EAST CORNER WAS A SUMMER-HOUSE (DEMOLISHED BY 1785) AND A BRIDGE GIVING ACCESS TO THE KITCHEN GARDEN ON THE OTHER SIDE OF THE KIRK LANE. BY 1668 THE GARDEN WAS IN USE AS A BOWLING GREEN. THE PRESENT ENTRANCE GATE FROM THE OUTER COURTYARD [1] WAS INSERTED IN 1740.

8. PARISH CHURCH

BUILT ABOUT 1140 BY THE DE MORTIMERS, OWNERS OF ABERDOUR CASTLE, AND DEDICATED TO ST FILLAN. THE NAVE AND CHANCEL ARE RARE EXAMPLES OF SCOTTISH ROMANESQUE ARCHITECTURE. THE SOUTH AISLE WAS ADDED ABOUT 1500. UNROOFED IN 1790 FOLLOWING THE BUILDING OF A NEW PARISH CHURCH IN THE HIGH STREET, IT WAS NICELY RESTORED IN 1925-6 AND RESURRECTED AS THE PARISH CHURCH.

Artist's bird's-eye view of Aberdour Castle from the north east.

The Architecture of Aberdour Castle

The Site

*T*he modern approach to Aberdour Castle is from the west, through the rebuilt seventeenth-century gateway, with its flanking gun-loops. In the Middle Ages, however, the original approach was from the north, but this was abandoned when the railway was built in 1890. Only then was the gateway relocated to its present position.

The site of the castle was of no great strength. On the west side the ground slopes quite steeply from the Dour Burn to the walls; to the south it has been reduced by the seventeenth-century terracing and to the north by the railway embankment. The old road linking West and East Aberdour skirted round the north side of the castle hill but the modern approach leads directly into what was the castle's outer courtyard in the seventeenth century. It was enclosed by the walled garden to the east, the castle to the south and the inner courtyard to the west. The wall of the inner courtyard is now reduced to its foundations but in the sixteenth century it was the outer wall of the castle and it is still possible to distinguish the entrance gate, the adjacent porter's lodge and the projecting round tower at the northern angle.

From the outer courtyard the north front of the castle can be viewed as a whole and can be seen to be the result not of a single, comprehensive plan but of a long process of alteration and expansion. This development took place in successive stages which constitute the western, central and eastern ranges of the castle as it stands today.

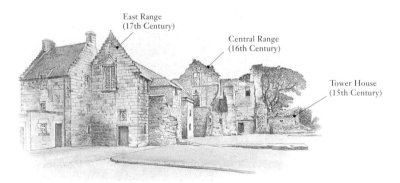

East Range
(17th Century)

Central Range
(16th Century)

Tower House
(15th Century)

The castle from the north east.

THE TOWER HOUSE

Towards the west end of the complex is the oldest part of the castle, the tower house. All that survives of this building is the basement and a substantial part of the south-east wall. It is a structure with a complicated history.

The tower house in fact began life as a two-storeyed building, possibly consisting of a large room, or hall, on the upper floor above a basement; hence the modern name given to this type of structure - hall house (see the reconstruction drawing on page 4). The original ground-floor entrance, later blocked, was through the eastern end of the south wall; its west jamb has a bar-hole. There was probably also a first-floor entrance above it, reached by an outside stair. Nothing can be said of the original internal arrangements of the ground floor except that it was unvaulted and lit by a series of slits. Three of these slits survive in the south wall. Little of the hall on the upper floor now remains. The most interesting features are the windows; the one facing west has stone seating, and that in the south wall once contained a double-lancet window of which the head now lies on the ground outside.

The stump of the tower house, with the castle well in the foreground.

A double-lancet window-head from the hall house.

This displaced window-head is one of several clues to the dating of this hall house, for it is similar to windows at nearby Inchcolm Abbey which are dated to about 1200. The cubical masonry of the walls is also indicative of such a date, being very like the masonry of nearby St Fillan's Church. Further confirmation of the early date is provided by the flat, clasping angle buttresses at either end of the east wall and the splayed base-course. These clues suggest that this hall house is one of the oldest standing masonry castles in Scotland.

An impression of the castle as it might have looked about 1500, drawn by Harry Bland.

At a later date, probably in the fifteenth century, the hall house was heightened and substantially redesigned internally to give it more the appearance of a tower house. An extra full storey and a garret were added to the top; the masonry of the 'new' work, of good quality ashlar, is clearly distinguishable from the original. Internally, the changes comprised the installation of a spiral stair at the south-east corner linking the various floors. At the same time, the basement was divided into two floors, a ground floor and an entresol. The ground floor now provided two rooms, one vaulted over in stone and the other ceiled with timber, the joists resting on a transverse member and the boards fitting into a raggle roughly cut in the walls. The original south entrance was blocked and a new entrance was cut through the east wall, giving direct access from the courtyard to the vaulted access passage. The arrangement of the accommodation at entresol level was similar to that below with the possible omission of the access passage. The east room was a vaulted **kitchen** with a large fireplace and a spacious aumbry, or cupboard, with wooden doors. The arrangement of the upper floors is now far from clear, but the evidence of the south-east wall and of a watercolour painted in 1836 (see the illustration on the inside front cover) show that above the first floor there was one main storey and a garret, both with wooden floors.

To the west of the tower house is the **service courtyard**. The ruined buildings there now date from the sixteenth century but very probably perpetuate an earlier arrangement. The buildings include a **brewhouse** and **bakehouse** with two large ovens.

THE CENTRAL RANGE

The central range of buildings, to the south and east of the tower house, was added in the later sixteenth century, probably by Regent Morton, to provide a more fitting residence; the old tower house was downgraded as a result. There had previously been a building on this spot, as the fragments at ground level, notably a door and window in the sixteenth-century kitchen, indicate. This was possibly a two-storeyed structure with a **great hall** on the first floor, for more lavish entertainment than might be provided within the confines of the tower house, above a service basement. The hall block and tower house had been linked by a spiral stair.

Morton's new building was a three-storeyed structure constructed of random rubble covered externally with a harl, or roughcast. The side facing south onto the gardens was quite plain but the east gable, which would have been the first part seen by visitors entering the castle courtyard, was ornamented by elaborate window surrounds (see the photograph on page 8), similar to those at other buildings associated with Morton like Edinburgh and Drochil castles. The new building continued to be linked to the old tower house by the **spiral stair**, suitably altered particularly at ground level where the new main entrance was created. A **second spiral stair** at the south-west corner of the new building gave rear access to and from the terraced garden.

Tower House

Central Range

East Range

Collapsed Tower House

The castle from the south west.

Internally the accommodation consisted of two main rooms on each floor connected by a passage running along the north side. At ground level the passage originally gave access to the courtyards to east and west, the inner courtyard and service courtyard respectively; the former doorway was later blocked off. The two rooms off the passage were a **kitchen** and **store room**, both vaulted. The oven in the kitchen fireplace was inserted in 1674.

The accommodation on the upper two floors provided separate **private apartments** for Morton and Lady Elizabeth. Each apartment comprised two main rooms, an **outer chamber** on the west (which was later referred to as a dining room) and an **inner chamber** on the east. A smaller room, or **closet**, formed from the east end of the north passage was entered off the inner chamber. The rooms would have been sumptuously furnished, particularly the inner chamber with its ornate, heavily-draped bed. Only the large windows and fireplaces survive to hint at their former grandeur.

The roof and top storey have been altered. Originally there was a pitched roof over the main rooms, a separate pitched roof over the passage and an independent conical roof over the main stair. The height of the main stair was subsequently increased and a pitched roof carried across from the tower house to a new gable built up on the south side of the passage. At the same time the pitched roof over the east part of the passage was removed and the main roof carried over the passage to the north wall. This arrangement increased the efficiency of the roof and added extra accommodation at the head of the stair and over the west end of the passage. A storey was also added to the turret which was converted into a stair to suit the new arrangement.

Morton's castle represented a big advance in comfort and convenience on the original tower house, although the latter continued to be used. The plan is unusual for a period when rooms usually connected directly with each other or with a stair.

An impression of how Regent Morton's inner chamber might have looked, drawn by Harry Bland.

The castle from the south east.

THE EAST RANGE

This range was built for William Morton, the sixth Earl; his initials - WEM for William, Earl of Morton - appear on the east gable (see the photograph on page 10). The range is L-shaped with a projecting **wing** at the south-east corner and the principal stair in the re-entrant angle. Two smaller **towers** project from the north front, the one an integral feature of the original structure, the other an early addition for which the moulding at gutter level had to be cut away.

The masonry of this extension is evenly coursed rubble, the gables are crow-stepped, the roofs tiled. The main roof was later reduced in height and the lintels of the windows at first-floor level lowered. The west tower, the chief feature of the north front and which contained an enriched window similar to that in the east gable, has been reduced almost to sill level. The original appearance can be deduced from the projecting wing where the roof-pitch and dormer windows have been restored.

Internally both the main block and the projecting wing were divided into three floors. At ground level the main block was divided into two by a pend connecting the inner courtyard with the terraced garden. One of the rooms was later used as a **stable** with lofts above.

The stable

The entire first floor of the main body of the range was occupied as a **gallery** which could be entered either from the central range, from the projecting wing or from the inner courtyard. Only the fine fireplace in the centre of the south wall survives to hint at the former glory of this the main room in the seventeenth-century castle. The whole appearance has been spoiled by alterations to windows and roof. The windows were taller, the roof higher and possibly concealed by a timber ceiling which may have been elaborately painted, and the walls panelled. Here the family displayed their portraits and entertained their guests. In 1647 the room contained 46 pictures and a great deal of furniture, including 13 chairs, 18 stools, a day bed, a harpsichord, a marble table and three cabinets. In the first-floor room in the projecting wing is a fine **painted ceiling**.

An impression of how the seventh Earl's gallery might have looked, drawn by Harry Bland.

THE GARDENS

Life in a castle was not as spartan as might appear today, and by the end of the Middle Ages many lordly residences had extensive pleasure grounds around them. The earliest mention of a garden at Aberdour is in 1540, although this may not have been the first on the site. Regent Morton, himself a keen gardener, probably laid out the present terraced garden to the south of the castle, and by 1650 they had been extended to the east and joined by a walled garden. Their survival provides important evidence for early garden layout in Scotland.

The full extent of the **terraced garden** was only rediscovered in the 1970s and plans are in hand to restore it (see the reconstruction drawing on page 3). It consists of four broad L-shaped walled terraces interlinked by flights of steps. On the level ground below the terraces in 1690 an orchard was laid out by Charles Liddel, the gardener, and planted with three dozen fruit trees, including peach and 'apricock'. At the furthest end of

The castle from the terraced garden.

The dovecot.

the garden from the castle is a beehive-shaped **dovecot** housing about 600 stone nesting-boxes. It probably dates from the end of the sixteenth century but there was an earlier dovecot for a charter of 1540 refers to the barony of Aberdour with its castle, fortalice, manor place, mills, fish-ponds, farms, parks, gardens, orchards, dovecots and rabbit warrens. The **Nether Mill** still survives beside the Dour Burn below the dovecot, and the excavations in the 1970s found what may have been rabbit warrens for a large pile of sand beside the dovecot may have been a 'pillow mound' in which rabbits were farmed.

The **walled garden**, a characteristic seventeenth-century feature, encloses an area of 1/2 hectare (about an acre) within walls almost 4 m high. The original entries are on the west from the terraced garden and on the east from the kirk lane. The pediments of both gateways are enriched, the former with the Douglas heart, the latter with the date 1632 and the monogram of William, Earl of Morton and his wife, the Countess Anne. The courtyard gate was inserted in 1740. A **summer-house** once projected from the south-east corner of the garden which in 1675 contained three chairs, a carpet, two kirk

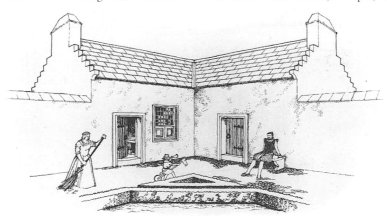

An impression of how the summer-house in the walled garden might have looked, drawn by Harry Bland.

cushions and a Bible. It had been demolished by 1785. Beside it there was a bridge connecting the walled garden with the **kitchen garden** on the other side of the lane. Some evidence for these features remains. The original layout of the garden is unknown but by 1668 it was a **bowling green**.

Contemporary seed lists give some idea of the vegetables, flowers and shrubs that were planted at the castle. In 1687 William Reid, an Edinburgh merchant, supplied vegetable seeds including leek, carrot, parsnip, radish, pea, cauliflower, scorzonera, turnip, spinach and lettuce. Flowers and other plants were supplied in 1691 by James Sutherland, one of the best known Scottish gardeners of his day, from the Physic Garden at Edinburgh, the forerunner of the present Royal Botanic Garden. The list included double yellow roses, Persian jasmine, lilac and honeysuckle, raspberries and strawberries, tamarisks, figs, medlars and double flowered cherries.

The monogram of William, seventh Earl of Morton, and the Countess Anne, carved in 1632 on the pediment over the east gate into the walled garden.

FURTHER READING

ON THE CASTLE:
W Ross *Aberdour and Inchcolm* (1885)
N Hynd and G Ewart 'Aberdour Castle Gardens', *Garden History*, II (1983), 93-111
J Gifford *Fife: The Buildings of Scotland* (1988), 60–4

ON THE DOUGLASES AND REGENT MORTON:
W Fraser *The Douglas Book* (1885)
G Donaldson *James V –James VII* (1976)

ON CASTLES GENERALLY:
S Cruden *The Scottish Castle* (1981)
C Tabraham *Scotland's Castles* (1997)